T0208869

The Poet, The Dove, and Spreading the Love

NOW THAT YOU'RE HERE, TO HEAR, YOUR SPECIAL, IT'S CLEAR

VOLUME I

MATTHEW HUNTER LARSEN

WESTBOW
PRESS®
A DIVISION OF THOMAS NELSON
& ZONDERVAN

This is a work is of prophetic poetry and a testimony of the author, given to the author by the pure intent, love and forgiveness of our Lord Jesus Christ and Our Heavenly Father. Our one true God, who loves us all. The author gives no guarantees that this works for everyone, only trusts to inspire. It works for the author and the author professes to be blessed and stay blessed. Amen.

WestBow Press books may be ordered through booksellers or by contacting:

WestBow Press
A Division of Thomas Nelson & Zondervan
1663 Liberty Drive
Bloomington, IN 47403
www.westbowpress.com
844-714-3454

Scripture quotations are taken from the Holy Bible, New Living Translation, copyright ©1996, 2004, 2015 by Tyndale House Foundation. Used by permission of Tyndale House Publishers, Carol Stream, Illinois 60188. All rights reserved.

ISBN: 978-1-6642-7081-7 (sc)
ISBN: 978-1-6642-7082-4 (hc)
ISBN: 978-1-6642-7083-1 (e)

Library of Congress Control Number: 2022912106

Print information available on the last page.

WestBow Press rev. date: 7/27/2022

1. Lives for Living and Speaking Out
What you've been given,

Landing onto something big.
Come with me and have a dig.

Your mind and heart are at the start.
Don't be surprised; begin this part.
Not everyone's been gifted in art.

2. Falling Forward

With each step, you'll grow.

Never look back;
Shine and flow.
Be prepared;
You already know.

This time here,
You're hitting the goal.

Lay it all down.
Speak from your soul.
Bring people back
Out of the hole.

Yesterday's history;
Tomorrow's a mystery.

Today's your place.
You stand in grace,
And the best about this
Is life you can face.

Be inspired,
Daily fed and fired.

Tune into life
And be rewired.

The mind's a place where
You will get tired.

Take pen to paper
And get out what's to be tried.

You're actually living,
Not the walking dead.

An elevating door
Is already ahead.

Are you called back home?
Take it and run.

Leave behind
All the pain and shame;
Hand to hand,
Start again.

You weren't left with no purpose;
It was only a test.
You know deep down
You're truly blessed,
Forever close and always at rest.

Isaiah 61
Is yours, my son.
Thank me now.
It's already done.

A changed mind,
An open heart,
Ready for a fresh, new start.

Things of the spirit
Are never apart.

Reclaim the kingdom;
It's declared and decreed.

Stand firm in truth;
Read love bleeds.

Keep God at the center;
He supplies your every need.

I'm not ignorant
Of Satan's foul lies,
For he is a father
Who always denies.

But here's the truth, and it always stands:
You're the one in God's hands.
So be strong and courageous.

Here's a wee reminder
Of what you already know:
God's number one
And always in control.

Have a wee look.
What do you see?
The sun is shining
With a fresh, new breeze.

It's time to pack, and don't look back.
Strong in the mind, you're now on track.

Dip in the river; we don't slack.
Keep your head up, and keep fighting back.

We can all say *why*;
You can't deny,
Even when things
Seem like they're passing by.

All of a sudden,
Your heart cries,
Forgetting the good
And believing the lie.

Get up, my child.
You're not denied.
Come to me
With arms open wide.
I'll be happy to give you
All treasures inside.

Endless promises;
No need to hide.
I've unconditional love
For you, my child.

More and more storms
Try to get in the way
The further you're going
With each new day.

So bring it on;
I'm always fresh,
Out to destroy
Any old flesh.

Embrace the race;
You're running with grace.

Keep doing your best,
And let God do the rest.

Broken focus—
Don't be scared to fail.

Success is waiting;
You're on the trail.

You'll become much stronger;
You've got the will.

Tunnel visioned—
Quit being still.

March great warriors
Up the hill.

Let light shine
For all to fill.

Reflect the image;
You're worth more than a bill.

Name it; claim it—
That's what's gonna come.

Speak with persistence
What's already done

While sitting back
And having fun.

The past is history.
There's no need to run.

Enjoy the moment;
Be thankful for one—

It's how you spend time
Under the sun.

Choose a life led by bread;
That's the truth—
You're always fed.

Loyalty and kindness—
Make them your gold chain.

Never let those leave
The chemicals in the brain.
Switch them on and turn them up.

As temperature is rising
And you step out of hiding,

Don't ever give in.
Little things seem big
When you're determined to win.

That's how you know
It's in line with the flow
And you're coming out strong.
Bright is the glow.

Pick yourself up off the floor.
You're right beside an open door.

Don't listen to lies.
They'll only have you hypnotized
Behind the eyes; it's no surprise.

Mind's in lockdown,
Forgetting who you are,
Made to achieve
As you always believe.

The chosen ones
Standing firm in truth
Know the end result:
Love always rules.

Every day's new.
Love's like glue.
It's everything about
What you wanna do.

Improving each moment,
The change is true.
Making it special,
We're chosen to.

Counting the memories
We spend with you,

They're cherished and loved,
Unlimited dove,
Set apart and received from above.

Love, mercy, and justice—
We hate wrongdoing.

Living in truth,
Walking with the youth,

Called and purified,
We're not denied,
Especially those people
Thinking they're disqualified.

The time will come;
You'll see the Son
Who shines like a diamond,
And you'll know he's the one.

God-given poet,
I'm here to show it,
Touching those who need to know it.
You've been given a gift;
Now it's time to bestow it.

Bold in the world,
Show your crown.
Take control; you're in this town.

All power and authority
Have been given to me.
I'm the chosen one,
And now you're gonna see
Everything's outta love
For you and me!

Seven keys of love
Straight from above.

In Revelation 3,
And I'm talking verse 8,
The Lord gives us
The keys to the gate.

We may have had little strength
But didn't deny his name,

For we know in our hearts
He's always the same.

Enter in, my child.
The battle's been won.

Walking out in faith,
Everything's done.

Shine bright like a diamond.
That's what we see.
All negativity has to flee.
Spring full of water
For you and me.

Let grace run its race; fully embrace.
You've entered into the family;
There is no second place.

Choose the destination
And pass the test.
Fight every time, and do your best.
Narrow out the roads,
And make a path for the rest.
Muscle on, young champ;
You know you're highly blessed.

Shalom to the home; Abba's on the throne.
It's already finished—freedom through the Son.

Shalom, shalom, speaking from home
To any dry places and worn-out bones.
We're here to say you will live this day.

This is what the Great Lord's done,
Brought you from death so your life's begun.

Shalom, shalom, we know our home.
Heaven's on earth, and love's given birth
To spread around and claim your crown.
Now you know the King's in town.

Never ever trust any sight.
Stay in direction.
Let faith keep you right.

Love's so strong
It's even gotta fight.
Keep on going; you're in top flight.

Speak and declare
You are made right
By the mighty power
Of Jesus Christ.

Slice up the pie;
I'll take some now.
Joy always comes
After the cry.

Made in the image
Uniquely of God,
Perfection built up
After a fall.

Taking the humble position,
Scrap the fame.
False identity
Will only drive you insane.

Expectation is normally the same.
Believe and receive—
Put in your name,
For after all,
You've had your pain.

We can all ask questions.
God, what happened there?
It's only eating us up,
Leaving despair.

We've gotta move on
And never give up.

You'll be in top form soon,
Bringing in the new,
Putting logs on the fire,
And keeping it true.

We've gotta reach out
And show these people

What life's all about,
Bringing hope beyond bars
Without any doubt.

Here's a one-time prayer:
Stand up and declare
Love breaks the chains
To set the captives free.
I'm in you,
And you're in me.

Comparison
Is the thief of joy,
Thinking you've found
Another lasting toy.

Searching for answers,
Your mind's in toil.
Just a few minutes later,
Your body's in boils,

Forgetting the good,
Being nasty and rude,
Before acknowledging
What's really true.

Now you know
What to do
When anything else
Seems tempting to you.

Yesterday's healed;
Tomorrow's hope.

Now that's the truth
And clearly spoke.

No longer bound
By chains and ropes,

You're free to be
Speaking things
You wanna see.

Counterfeits come,
Unknown to some,
Saying that you're
Truly the one.

Looking back in despair,
Taking drugs and didn't care.

But forget all that;
It's nothing to compare.
The Lord chose me, and you will declare

His faithful promise has come to pass;
You've life to the full,
And that's everlasting too.

Only for love
We wouldn't pull through.
You've lifted us up
To be with you.

Friday night, rainbows bright
On all the promises made in life.

Living it large,
Don't go by sight.
Faith takes you anywhere,
Day or night.

Walking and declaring,
So hold on tight.
It may seem slow,
But it's worth the fight.

You already know;
Trust the process.
You're gonna be all right.

Only took a seat;
It may have looked like defeat,
But realistically,
It's all in de feet.

Bringing new change
To blow your minds,
This positive gift
Is flowing through rhythms.

Taking broken pieces
And mending lost souls
In times of trouble,
Making open wounds closed.

It's time we get together
And rip off the grave clothes,
Spreading the love.
It's all coming soon.

Keep hope high;
Forget the rope.
Make sure you know
These lyrics are spoken.

It's written well clear,
So do not fear
Another one for now;
Your vision is here.

Rebirth from heaven,
We can't be stopped.
Supernatural testimonies
Are unlocked.
Great is the timer
On the Almighty's clock.

Always becoming
What they say you can't,
Defending the chance,
You're at the top—
No limits in place.
You're never alone
When running the race.

Who's gonna stop
If you're allergic to excuses?
Bow only for Jesus,
For he is the King.
Christ is Lord, and all will see
He loves us so much.
You're reading this with me.

You're a child of God.
You will know
It doesn't matter
Where you go.

Keep that smile,
Keep that glow
Because you're still a champ
And we all know.

Remember the time
Being creative was prime.
You'll never lose your touch;
Keep that in mind.

It's time for an upgrade
Right about now.

You're still so young
And filled with dreams.

You've already got
Everything you need
Without even knowing
You're at full speed.

Allow your mind to drift away
Somewhere peaceful, and let it stay.

Don't get distracted by what they say.
You're living life in a very unique way

With a shepherd to guide you
Each and every day.

Making room for the new
Love doesn't play.

No matter the pain,
Remember the name
Jesus Christ is always the same.
Rejoice in the now;
There is no shame.

Mind prepared
For greater change

Encouraging the ones
New in faith,

Building and helping
All in need,

Any moment now,
Get ready to leave,
Pack your bags,
And go where I lead.

Everything else
Is all in me.

You're already healed and sealed;
It's done indeed.

Glory to the Father.
Through the Son,
The Spirit fell and life begun.

Healing came,
Prosperity too.
Springing forth,
You're in the new.

Now all authority
Belongs to you
Because I believe
I'll claim all these.

Most importantly,
The work is done
Giving thanks
For every promise
Under the sun.

In this life,
You're gonna have storms.

Knowing who you are and bouncing to the stars,
Filling in the gaps and breaking through the bars,

Aim beyond the sky, and dance for now;
You know where you're going with arms held high.

Spread out them wings and begin to fly.
Life's full of treasures;
Only believe you can.
Matthew 19:26
Is in your hand.

Jesus looked at them intently and said,
Humanly speaking, it is impossible.
But with God everything is possible,
Matthew 19:26 (NLT).

Don't be limited
By the lyrics that I speak.
In this message,
You'll know you're not weak.

As time goes on,
You're gonna get strong.
Now put the foot down;
There's nothing wrong.

Raised up in violence,
What do you expect?
With a heart like a lion,
We always fight back.

Give it a go;
It's a chance to grow.
Stop worrying about the future,
And go with the flow.

Love's so deep
You'll never run out.
Let it flow free;
It's always about.

Follow no idol.
Without any doubt,
You're here for a reason.
It's due this season.

Trust the process
And
Keep killing the flesh,

Leaving behind all that stress,
Looking to the future
While doing your best.

Live up or give up;
It's happening either way.
It's always your choice
Each and every day.

Stand firm in believing
Whatever you say.
Trust the process
Up, up, and away.

Don't even think
What if, what may.
Keep your focus real steady
Knowing the way,

Ready and prepared
For this new day.

The language barrier
That clearly needs broke
Walking in darkness
Without any hope

Until one day
Great love spoke,
Now in a position
To throw down the rope.

Step outside.
Open your cells.
Do you not hear
The ringing bells?

We already know
Your own gut tells,
So get up, little soldier,
And speak all is well.

Spread your wings
And
Begin to fly
Never in doubt; God doesn't lie.

Here to say
You can't deny
Living out love
Coming in with a flood.

Never alone,
God's on the throne.
Straight from heaven
The gift of the dove
Spirit, lead
Fearless above.

You've all heard
What's clearly true:

It's OK
To not always be you.

Sometimes in life,
We all need space.

Just get back up
And
Run the race,

Knowing that with grace,
You're coming first place.

I'm coming back
For everything that's mine.

God, give us life,
Creating new wine.

Forgetting the past,
It's all behind.

No worries
For the future,
You're present now.

Do what you love.
Let your light shine.

When you realise this,
You're in your prime,

Breaking the chains
Every time.

Take my hand
Knowing you can.

Nothing's impossible.
The Great I Am

Speaking out words,
That's hitting your land,

Shaking of the dust,
Raising out your hand.

This one's for the youth.
Believe me, it's truth.

Knowing your worth,
Don't try; just be,
Flowing and glowing
For all to see.
And
That one there's
Always free.

Living through a pandemic,
Staying in touch,
That's real and reality.

I'm feeling your pain
But still, young one,
It's love that wins again.
Here, here, there is no shame.
This life here isn't a game.

Sweet dreams to society,
Shalom to the melody.

Bringing hope and life
That's stronger than the bite,

Freeze the doubt;
We young soldiers
Will always live it out!

For the weak and weary,
Come and get rest.

Under God's wings,
You're protected and blessed,
Shielded and provided,
Forever dressed.

Ready to go,
You've been through the test,

Prejudicing good fruits,
And
Grown deep roots.
The doors are open.
Come fill your boots.

Bringing life back
To the very start,
It's always a choice—
Light or dark.

Deep are the roots
Ascending from heaven.
Come fill your boots.

Laughing is contagious,
But so is your smile.
Fill me up; I'm ready now.

We're made the same
Under the sun.
Never forget
You're the one.

Love's the key.
All will see
The heart flowing
For you and me

Lifted high
In this new season,
Speaking life
To our generation.

Vibes are tribes.
Surprise, surprise,
Everything in life
Has its times,

Ready for the change
That's gonna blow your minds.

Home is your heart.
Trust the art,
Grab the paintbrush,
And
Make a start—

Great opportunity.
Listen, you're smart,
Fearlessly living.
Two ears make a heart.

We young ones
Sure do have the art.
When one becomes whole,
We're never apart.

Ears start the heart, and you're the art.

Humble and kind,
God's full access
To blow my mind.

Unexpected miracles
Happen all the time.

Life's improving daily,
Landed into prime,

Loving with a passion,
Bringing in new rhymes,

Ripping down the lies,
And
Wiping tears of your eyes.

Never forget
The final prize.

Does any among you
Want to be wise?
Then keep your mouth
From telling lies.

No matter the circumstances,
Low or high,
Bite the tongue
And wave goodbye.

Watch what happens
When your spirit flies.

Lifted high,
Wings spread wide.

The best is here,
And it's very clear.

Lord, have your way
In and through me
Each new day.

Come in, Holy Spirit.
Wash me clean.
Help me conquer
What isn't for me,

All my days
Honouring your ways
With great delight
Shining so bright.

Come in more and make it right.
I surrender all
From morning to night,

Believing the truth,
Trusting your Word,
Walking in spirit,
And knowing true worth.

Surely, you knew
This was a test.
Every distraction
Tried its best.

Wavering thoughts
Were put to death
After the truth
Hit home to rest.

An outpouring for you,
It's new and true.
Nothing's impossible.
You're royalty too.

God, there's so much happening.
It's trying to lead us astray

Though we're reminded of your promises
Each and every day.

If it's not happening now,
That's OK
Because you know better.
You always make a way.

The faithful keeper
Has the final say.

We thank you, Lord,
For this new day.

Talk about beauty
All inside,
The realest gifts
Never to hide.

Overflowing in life and walking the way,
It's a brand-new start, and you're here today.

Eyes are being opened.
Now you see
Favour and love
Will always chase me.

I'm very thankful
For what's left behind,
Mind completely blowing
At this point now.

So spend it wise.
You know the prize:
A true legend
Never dies.

Setbacks are comebacks,
So bring it on.

The Lord's almighty,
And he's the one.

Starting from victory,
Here's the song.
If you know you're blessed,
Feel free, sing along.

Take the truth,
And learn from youth.

No weapon will prosper
Under our roof
Says the Lord
Who's mighty and strong.

Heaven's armies
Are coming along.

Bad times don't last;
You're not downcast.

The enemy always tries
To bring up your past.

He's all bark and no bite,
Trying to keep you
From living the life.

Let him roar all he wants,
But he's in for a fight
Because God's already said it:
You'll be all right.

This is one
You're clearly gonna know:

Nothing stopping God,
Blessings always flow.

Remember what's real,
Keeping the goal.

Some things in life
Have a glow.

What you set your mind on
Will always grow,
So take my hand and let it go.

Let's think big.
That's what God wants—
Taking limitations off.
And stop saying you can't.

The vision's very clear;
It's everything you want.

An unpredictable poet,
You already know it.

Wisdom will flow;
I'm here to show it,

Doing things
As you bestow it.

Timing is everything,
Like 3, 6, 9.

Only God's in control
All the time.

The keys to all doors
And there's nothing behind

Raised up for such a time.
Can't wait to see your face
As you always shine.

And walking in tune,
You're going far soon.

So don't quit in the dip.
You're doing so well
In this adventurous trip

While doing your bit
And always keeping her lit.

Your habits, temptations, desires, and means—

I know what'll bring you joy
Beyond your wildest dreams.

Loving God with all your heart
Is what satisfies your needs.
The wanting to please everyone—
Why can't it just be me?

My love for you
Is wide and far.
It outnumbers every star.

You've even got awakened
To shoot past the limitation.

So go and show the world you're in
The greatest love to ever win
With my cleansing blood
For all of sin.

Love the letter for the better.

Action in attraction,
It's all around.

The caterpillar has its rebirth
Up from the ground.

Yellow, green, blue, and white,
It's for you and me,
So hang on tight.

Making things new,
You're pulling through.

Spiritual ones know
These messages are true,

Divine connections
From heaven to you—
Given the sign when you need it too?

Hope, prosperity,
And transformation
Coming through
With everything else
That's all true.

You're going far in life
With inner wealth.

The rebirth wasn't easy.
Now you see clear.
Standing out from the rest,
You're entering the best.

That's another time
When everyone will look,
Standing in awe,
The haters all shook.

You may feel trapped
All in the mind,
And
It might seem like
It's taking some time.

But what's loving and true
Is coming to you,

Breaking through the bars,
And
That's real love for you.

So take your time
To learn and grow.

You're in this position,
And it's OK to know.

Chosen from the very start—
In Jeremiah chapter 1 verse 5,
It's clearly said, and never apart,
Created perfectly in the womb,
That's from the first start.

Thank you, Lord,
For being so faithful and true,
Calling me out of that dark tomb.

Big surprise coming through,
Spreading the love
Straight to you.

Bringing in the new
Mind power and God's will too,
Nothing's impossible,
Always pulling through.

Breathe it in and live it out,
Life to the full.
You're being resurrected.
Everything's new.

There's hoping and wishing,
Will it happen again?
Tomorrow's not promised.
Life's not a game

To live it without thinking
And having no shame.

Lifting others up
Regardless of name,

We're all in this world
And made the same.

I'm in you;
You're in me.

Realise this, and you'll be free.

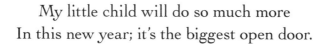

My little child will do so much more
In this new year; it's the biggest open door.

The things you'll see me do are all because I love you.
You'll spread your wings and go up high
Looking out for one another, aiming to the sky,

Going through life and speaking the truth,
Pulling each one up outta the muck,
telling the facts; don't ever give up.

The pain you feel, the torture to steel
Won't always have a place; I know where you'll be.

From the beginning of time, I made you to shine
Because in the end, you'll always be mine.

A little more open, and just be you.
I'm the guide to your day; I always pull through.

You've learned so much, keeping in touch.

With an attitude of gratitude, my love hits you hard.
There was no coincidence. I brought you this far.

Look up, my child, beyond the star.
I am the Creator. It's Jesus, your Saviour.

Hold on to me, and flow so free.
Anything that's negative, all has to flee!

29 December 2020

Always be thankful
For where you're at now
Because you know the test
Produces the best,

Coming out like a diamond
Shaped and dressed,
Shining and refining
In the process.

There're not that many
Willing to rest.

Know your worth,
And
Don't settle for less.

Slingshot and five stones
Hitting the bones.

Grace rewrote my story.
I know my home.

My Father isn't moving.
The King's on the throne.

Now that's a battle;
It's already done.

Everything belongs
To you, my son.

Don't look back.
The victory's won.

Shalom forever.
Love's the one.

Just woke up,
Reminded of the will
Pursuing great warriors
Up the hill.

They're strong and courageous.
They're born to win.

Living this day
In the very best way—
Live to the full
Extended version of you.

Tomorrow's new doors,
But you're here now.
Again, live to the full,
Living out the new
While the mind is being
Daily renewed.

Faith over fear,
Seeing really clear—
Is everything an illusion?
Think about that.
Now I'm here!

Everything you dreamed
Is sitting in a box,
Waiting for the right time
For the goods to be unlocked.

It's everything you need.
You've even got the key—
A little bit of faith—
All for you to see
That things are working out
All for you and me.

People on their deathbeds
Are dying for a chance,
Begging and weeping.
Wake up and start to dance.

You're only getting better,
So pull it together—
A little reminder
That you've got another chance.

Say it, share it, always declare it—
Mindset of a warrior, and that's how it goes.

Taking on anything,
Remember who's in control.

Let's not forget the real golden goal:
Living with love and showing the role.

Now it's time; there is no show
Because the comeback is greater
Than you'll ever know.

Humbled to say this is the way
Joined with the one—
Bring on the day.

Blessed to be a blessing, and that's a fact.
You are made right; it's time to act.
Keep moving forward, and don't ever look back.

Do you really care
What the devil has to say,
Bringing up the past
As if it's not a new day?

You make me laugh.
Now get on your way.

Believe in the truth;
It's imparted from youth.

I am loved beyond measures,
Protected, and blessed.

I'll go through the fire
Because God's got the rest.

So listen real careful:
You're passing the test,

Coming out pure gold,
Purifying what's best.

Father like son, you are the one
Chosen before the earth begun.

Looked after with care,
Now claim your chair;
In watchful arms, God's always there.

The size of a mustard seed is all it takes.
Then the faith starts growing and weeds start blowing.

Arise, little champ, and go where I'm showing,
Casting down strongholds
That were held in the mind.
The light is shining.
Forget what's behind.

Getting in flow
With eyes that glow,
Now it's time to let them know.

Love opens up.
Don't ever give in.
Picked with the wise,
You're born to win,

Steady and ready,
Leaving your mark.
In with the new
And outta the dark,

Where all a picture
Image of spark
Filled with compassion
And killing distraction.

I am the one
Who is your protection.
Thank you, God.
You're pure perfection.

Feeling numb and wanna run—
Is your mind playing games
And it's just not fun?

Honestly, friend,
I get where you're really coming from.

Being isolated, and family isn't there,
You need to know this:
There're people who actually care.

So all the voices and the doubts
Are gonna have to go.
They just don't belong here.
Love is now your home.

Shalom to the home.
Ask yourself the question,
Who's on the throne

Fighting your battles?
So just be still.
Keep pushing forward.
It's God's goodwill.

In perfect time,
You're gonna shine
Inside and out,
Making new wine.

Trust the divine.
Love takes time,
For after all,
You're always mine.

We sometimes forget
God's got the final say
And he made us all
In a very special way.

I know things may be hard,
And I'm talking right now
As you think you're on your own.
But always remind yourself
That you, dear, aren't alone.

You've got so much to say.
You're even reading this today.
Now that's a little hope
That's always gonna stay.

You're valuable and loved.
It's going to turn out just fine,
Better than what you're thinking.
It's gonna blow the mind.

So remember this season
Because you're worth every dime.

Mental health issues,
While needing some tissues,

Don't anyone understand.
We're all in the same land
Helping one another
Always if you can.

Take great joy
By holding out your hand,

Being deeply reminded
When lifting someone up

We're all here for a reason,
And it's time we came together
For this new season.

I just can't explain
Exactly what's going on.

The rebirth was scary.
I started to worry.

Being woken up
After many years,
There goes the suffering
While wiping away the tears.

The comebacks
Always greater
Than any of your fears,

And the goodness of God
Will be multiplying
All the years.

The wake-up's happening now

While many sit back
And you can't deny.

Focus on your future
Tunnel-visioned eye.

Letting go of limitations,
You're pushing through the sky.

There're gonna be some
Who question how.

Just don't buy into it.
You're free from now.

Not everything's gonna go your way
Passing through this new day.

Surprises filled and plugged into power
Opening up, you're going far.

Driving by in the AMG,
It's white and black,
Also clearly written:
Don't ever look back.

Something new from me to you—
There's nothing at all that love can't do.

What's really impossible?
And that one's true.

With God, you know
You're always pulling through.

To avoid any correction
Misleading direction,

Searching through history,
Looking for protection—

Is it all one way
With many astray?

Out for number one,
They're always gonna say,

"Take care of yourself
And have a nice day."

Though my mind's wired different,
I don't tend to play.

I've a heart for these people
Who need hope in every way.

Why oh why
Don't you just try?

Give it a go; you never know.
While learning to dance,
In rain or snow,

That's when things
Will start to show.

Manifesting showers
And becoming a light,
Blessings are here
Day and night.

Make it reality
As you grow.

The promise always stands;
Go with the flow.

Don't be held back
By what you can't control.

Holy Spirit filled,
I know I always am
Coming in fast.
So you can take off your mask,
Lighting things up
That were all downcast,
Speaking out life and paving a path.

There're always better days.
Listen and pray;
What the Lord says
Is coming your way.

Be cheerful and kind
One day at a time.
Rest in the promise
With grace that's honest.

In times of trouble,
God always pulls through.
Keep holding on
And trusting in him too
Because the one who is love
Is faithful and true.

Jesus came to give us life
To have it to the full.
Even in dark valleys,
The Lord will guide me through.

Great is his faithfulness.
His love never ends.

Knowing that I'm never alone,
My heart belongs to you.

Accepting all the goodness,
You've been patient the whole way through.
I will count on you for all my days,
Living out only what is true.

Words just can't describe
How blessed I am in you,
And anytime when I get stuck
In doing things my own way,

You've never left me hanging.
You always make a way.

When things seem like they're falling away
Piece by piece, your body says
Lie down, great warrior.
Have some rest.
Nearly everything in life
Comes with a test.

Keep on top as problems drop,
Knowing that all will finally stop
And in the end, you'll come to clap.

So, for now, be strong and lift your hat.
It won't be long
Until you're back on top.

Learning the will and mastering the skill
To be remembered,
I always will.

Becoming the one,
Watch and learn.
With Christ in you,
It's always done.

There's always power
In want you think.
Keep on loving;
Let worries sink.

Never give up and never give in.
You were made perfect
To always *win*.

Share your kindness.
Be strong in all you do
Because in the end,
Showing love
Will always pull through.

You're one of a kind.
Believe me, it's true.
Set your goals high
And know I love you.

Everything's possible.
Keep that in mind
When you're feeling down
Anytime.

Focus on now,
What all you can do
With the boldness of a warrior.
The champ is in you.

There're always lies
Trying to keep you down,
But know the truth
That sets you free.
Everything is possible;
Only believe.

When you hear the words
"Live your life,"

You can bubble up.
Give me the mic.

I'll tell you facts
About living out truth.

Is it easier to say,
"Live this way,"
Or
To set the example
Each and every day?

Well, then,
Do what's in your heart.
You know the ending
From the start.

You've just put another smile
On the Great King's heart.

Love's the key.
Come join with me;
Joy is now and we're being set free.

Peace like a river
Flows from thee,

Patience with endurance
Growing fruit on the tree.

Kindness and goodness
Will follow you and me,

For the Lord is faithful and gentle
Wherever we go.

Self-control is learned;
That's how we roll.

God is love, and this I know,
For the Bible tells me so.

Wide are the blessings;
Deep is the love.

Glory to God
Our Father above.
In Christ, we live;
Jesus is King.

Sharing with faith
That God's in me,
Before we knew,
He carried us through.

No longer a slave
To any abuse,
Call on the Lord;
He speaks only truth.

The victory's won;
Our debt was paid,
Making all things new.
Before you were born,
God already knew.

In his righteousness, you stand
In favour that's true.
Whatever is good
Is a free gift too.

Be a blessing to many
Because I chose you.

Breakthrough after breakthrough
Like never before,

Whatever is negative
Will be shown the door
Not to come back anymore.

Everything destructive
Will all be flushed out,
And there isn't even
One single doubt.

It's all for you,
So, whatever your mind's saying,
Don't always pull through.

Go with the heart,
And know you're loved too.

Forgiveness is key.
Believe and see.

All is well.
Abide in me.

Persistence in spirit,
Led by truth,

Slaying down giants,
You're daily empowered too,

The strength of Christ
Conquering through.

Arise each day.
Lord, have your way.

The grace of God
Is here to stay.

So, whatever you're facing,
Take it day by day.

Live it.
Breathe it.
Always believe it.

Shaking of doubts,
Level things out.

Words like honey
Just flow from the mouth.

Sweeter the juice,
More is produced.
Come fill your boots;
Liven and given,
Growing deep roots.

At just the right time,
I'll be back for mine.

Hang on in there.
I'm making new wine.

You're gonna be
Super surprised,

For in this month,
It's harvest time,

Reaping after sowing
Without really knowing.

God's got it sorted.
Let go of controlling.

And there's nothing else
For you to do.
The payment for your life
Was made in full!

Just let that loving truth
Overwhelm you,
And
Always give thanks
In all you do.

Here's a wee story that will hit home:
Do you feel abandoned and all alone?

You know they care,
But sometimes, it feels
Like they're just not there.

You're trying your best
While being hit with the rest.

Is this the time
Where you start to dig deep?

For I'm sure at this point,
You're feeling weak,
Thinking to yourself,
Is this my last sleep?

The head hits the pillow,
But your mind's not sweet.

I'm just telling you the truth.
It's the positive changes
Coming in your life.
Because God's in control,
You're gonna be all right.

This world that we're in
Is coming to a close.

Give your full potential
As you are called and chose,

Keeping eyes to the north,
And watch giants be told

One word of love
As life unfolds.

In the supernatural,
You're young and bold.

Start dancing now
Because they already know

That you're hand-picked
And God's in control.

Home is exactly
Where you feel at peace,
A place to rest
And
Trusted deep

With the Holy Spirit
That talks so sweet.
Hearing the sound,
It's your own heartbeat.

Keeping in touch,
This walk is a must.
Live in divine
While learning to trust,

Staying connected
Like rhythms and rhymes.
Making real diamonds,
Now it's time.
Under the pressure,
You're doing just fine

Because you've already got
What most people wish.

Always be thankful
For every bliss,
And embrace the grace
With a beautiful kiss.

It's time for an upgrade
Right about now.

You think you're old?
Not in my eyes.

You're still so young
And filled with dreams.

You've already got
Everything you need.

Without even knowing,
You're at full speed.

Open it up and have a read.

Arise, arise.
Open your eyes.

The light has come;
Bright are the skies.

Blow off the cobwebs,
And pray for the spies.

Don't let what's going on
Come in and hide.

Get it together,
And shake off the pride,

For yet again,
You thought you died.

Never forget
God pulled you through.

Now it's time,
All things made new.

Arise, great warrior.
I'm always with you.

Faith lives out
Deaf to any doubt,

Walking in
Abundant grace
With Jesus always
In first place,

Taken by the right hand
Into a promised land,

Speaking and declaring
The Great King
Has a plan.

In and out,
No messing about,

Get the job done
And do not doubt.

Life's going forward,
So live it out.

Write the vision clear
For you to hear.

From this point on,
It's drawing near.

Love and get along,
For you're special, my dear.

Start living life
Without any fear.

You're in God's hands.
Now it's crystal clear.

Indecisive in what to do,
But this I know:
I'll always pull though.

Might feel weak,
But I know I'm strong.

So, if you're unsure,
Just carry on.
Trust the process;
It always turns out best.

Interest? Deep down inside,
You have a crown.
Keep marching on
Pound by pound.

You're born to win,
So take your stand
Crushing the chickens,
With your bare hands.

Speaking it out,
Nothing's impossible.
Give me a shout,
Headphones on,
When you hear the doubt.

The Great I Am is always about.

You may be under pressure,
But *this I know*:
That's how diamonds are made.
You're always gonna grow.

It may be tight
In the here and now
Because of the feelings
That are just passing by.

It's only a season.
Remember the reason.

For the one true plan
That's out of your hand,
*Just keep trusting
In the Great I Am.*

Be still and be thankful.
You're not going downhill.
It may feel slow
In fulfilling the will.

Though the time is coming,
It'll happen so fast.

Your head's gonna spin
With so many blessings that last

Minute after minute,
Breaking free
From the past.

It'll all be worth it
With an everlasting laugh.

Come take your *place*.
Put a smile on your *face*

Because things in *life*
Won't always be *here*.

One thing *remains*;
It's love and it's *clear*.

Taken by the *ear*
And
Speaking to the *fear*,

Listen to your *heart*.
This is a brand-new *start*.

From this day *forward*,
Remember the *art*.

Good morning, good day
Wherever in the world
You're led to stay.

Take a minute and pause,
Giving thanks to our God
That gives us a way.

Put your hand on your heart;
You can feel that beat.

You're hearing this message,
Good news to the street,
Being freed from all deceit.

So get up and go.
Stay connected in life.

Plugged into flow
With the Lord as your shepherd,
His light will always show.

You're standing here
Reading this clear.
You've got a great purpose,
So have no fear.
Always remember
That God is near.

You gotta get up
And
Stand firm on your feat

Because you know this life
Is short and sweet.

Nothing's impossible.
Deaf to defeat!

Every day's new.
Your love's like glue,
And it's all about what you do.

So bring in the vibe
And spread it out wide
While surfing and grinding
Through life's open tide,
And you'll realise soon
It's all inside.

Keeping in mind
There are other people too,
A timing for everything,

Always stay true
And keep being you
Because we all know
You're pretty cool.

*You're loved, you're listening, and it's very clear
There is a good reason that you're still here!*

There's always power
In what you think.
Keep pushing forward;
You're not gonna sink.

Be single-minded
In all you do,
Knowing that your love
Will always pull through.

Because we're all made unique
And you know it's true,
Always enjoy
Your life to the full.

Any doubt or fear
That's trying to whisper in your ear?
Let go of this person
That's reading right here.

I speak life over you,
And it's gonna come true.
Keep moving on;
Set your goals high too.

From this day forward,
You shall arise
Crying in joy.
It's no surprise
You've been down for so long.
Now open your eyes.

Always be thankful;
Bright is the sky.
There's only one true God
You can't deny.

This is the time.
Forgetting what's behind,
This revelation knowledge
Is sure to blow your mind.

Shrewd and intelligent,
The Lord will impart
All with understanding
Asking for a start.

That's when you'll discover
A freshly open heart
Learning and listening.
Oh … this is proper art.

19 December 2021

Be still and be thankful.
You're not going downhill.
It may feel slow
In fulfilling the will.

Though the time is coming,
It'll happen so fast.

Your head's gonna spin
With so many blessings that last

Minute after minute,
Breaking free
From the past.

It'll all be worth it.
It's time to laugh.

Grind through
The challenges of life
That come in your way
Day or night.

Always remember it's only a test
Making you stronger and stronger,
Purifying what's best.

Life can be hard
At times for us too;
The chosen ones know
☺ this is true.

Printed in the United States
by Baker & Taylor Publisher Services